I0815509

ANIMAL GROUPS
Bee Hives
by Rachel Grack
BLASTOFF! 3 READERS
BELLWETHER MEDIA • MINNEAPOLIS, MN

Blastoff! Readers are carefully developed by literacy experts to build reading stamina and move students toward fluency by combining standards-based content with developmentally appropriate text.

Level 1 provides the most support through repetition of high-frequency words, light text, predictable sentence patterns, and strong visual support.

Level 2 offers early readers a bit more challenge through varied sentences, increased text load, and text-supportive special features.

Level 3 advances early-fluent readers toward fluency through increased text load, less reliance on photos, advancing concepts, longer sentences, and more complex special features.

★ **Blastoff! Universe**

Reading Level

Grade K

Grades 1–3

Grade 4

This edition first published in 2026 by Bellwether Media, Inc.

Library of Congress Cataloging-in-Publication Data

LC record for Bee Hives available at: https://lccn.loc.gov/2025018373

Editor: Suzane Nguyen Designer: Brittany McIntosh

Printed in the United States of America, North Mankato, MN.

Table of Contents

Sweet Bees

Honeybees are known for their sweet honey. They are important **pollinators**.

Honeybees live in places like forests and cities around the world. Inside each buzzing hive, a **colony** of bees is busy at work.

Inside the Hive

Honeybees build hives in **hollow** trees. They also build hives in the gaps of rocks and walls. They make hives from beeswax.

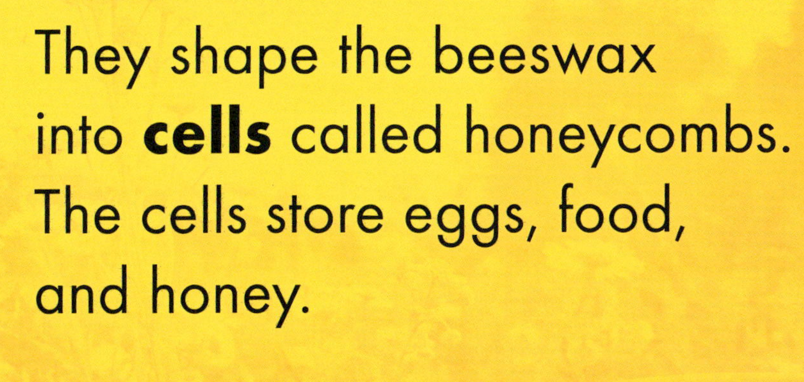

They shape the beeswax into **cells** called honeycombs. The cells store eggs, food, and honey.

cells

Colonies can have up to 80,000 bees. Most are female worker bees. They build the hive and look for food.

The queen bee runs the hive and lays eggs. Male bees are called drones. They **mate** with the queen.

Honeybees use **chemical signals** to **communicate**. The queen's signals keep worker bees busy. Worker bees' signals warn other workers of danger.

Worker bees do the waggle dance. The dance tells other workers where to find food.

Tending the Hive

Worker bees gather food for the hive. They use their straw-like tongues to suck **nectar** from flowers.

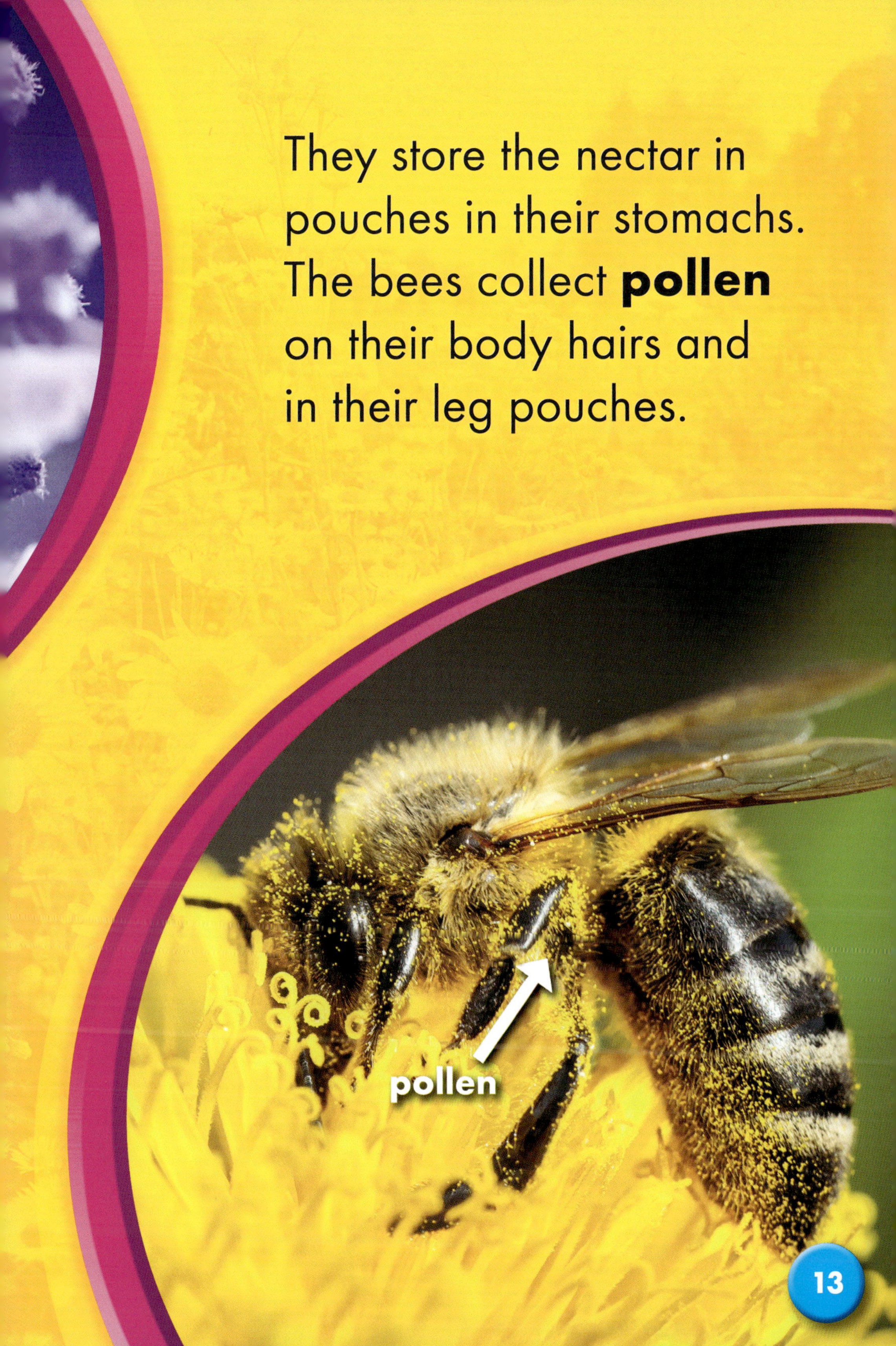

They store the nectar in pouches in their stomachs. The bees collect **pollen** on their body hairs and in their leg pouches.

Worker bees carry food back to the hive.

They mix nectar and pollen with honey. This makes bee bread. It feeds the whole colony.

bee bread

Honeybee Diet
honey
bee bread

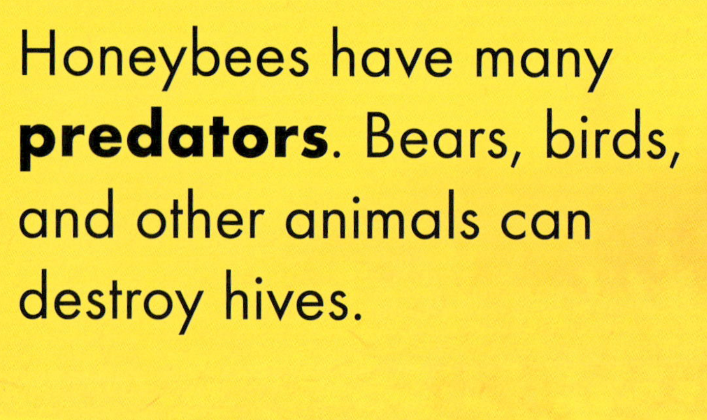

Honeybees have many **predators**. Bears, birds, and other animals can destroy hives.

Honeybees give off chemical signals when in danger. Worker bees rush to help. They sting anything that comes too close.

Bee Eggs

Queens can lay around 2,000 eggs in one day. They lay eggs in the honeycomb cells.

Fertilized eggs become worker bees or queens. Unfertilized eggs become drones.

Worker bees care for the **brood**. They work for the hive when they are grown.

Queen eggs get **royal jelly**. These bees grow larger and can lay eggs. Someday, one of them will become the new queen!

Glossary

brood—the developing eggs, larvae, and pupae of bees

cells—small areas in bee nests and hives that hold food and young bees

chemical signals—chemicals given off by animals that cause certain behaviors in other animals

colony—a single bee family made up of a queen, drones, and worker bees

communicate—to send and receive information

fertilized—relating to female eggs that have been joined with a male cell

hollow—empty through the middle

mate—to join together to make young

nectar—a sweet liquid found in plants, especially flowers

pollen—a fine dust that helps plants make seeds

pollinators—animals that spread pollen from one flower to another

predators—animals that hunt other animals for food

royal jelly—a creamy food created by worker bees that is fed to female bees that may become queen bees

To Learn More

AT THE LIBRARY

Forest, Christopher. *Beehives*. New York, N.Y.: AV2 by Weigl, 2020.

Pettiford, Rebecca. *Honeybees*. Minneapolis, Minn.: Bellwether Media, 2025.

Woods, Alix. *Bees*. Kent, U.K.: Ruby Tuesday Books, 2025.

ON THE WEB

FACTSURFER

Factsurfer.com gives you a safe, fun way to find more information.

1. Go to www.factsurfer.com.
2. Enter "bee hives" into the search box and click 🔍.
3. Select your book cover to see a list of related content.

Index

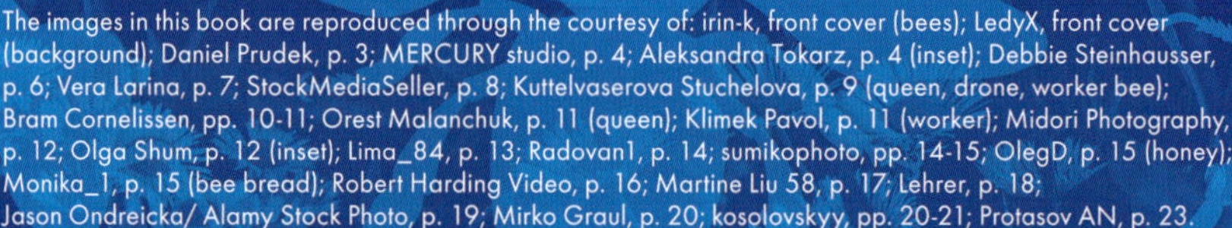

The images in this book are reproduced through the courtesy of: irin-k, front cover (bees); LedyX, front cover (background); Daniel Prudek, p. 3; MERCURY studio, p. 4; Aleksandra Tokarz, p. 4 (inset); Debbie Steinhausser, p. 6; Vera Larina, p. 7; StockMediaSeller, p. 8; Kuttelvaserova Stuchelova, p. 9 (queen, drone, worker bee); Bram Cornelissen, pp. 10-11; Orest Malanchuk, p. 11 (queen); Klimek Pavol, p. 11 (worker); Midori Photography, p. 12; Olga Shum, p. 12 (inset); Lima_84, p. 13; Radovan1, p. 14; sumikophoto, pp. 14-15; OlegD, p. 15 (honey); Monika_1, p. 15 (bee bread); Robert Harding Video, p. 16; Martine Liu 58, p. 17; Lehrer, p. 18; Jason Ondreicka/ Alamy Stock Photo, p. 19; Mirko Graul, p. 20; kosolovskyy, pp. 20-21; Protasov AN, p. 23.